P9-DNC-927

I Love
Dogs and Puppies

Nicola Jane Swinney

Sandy Creek
NEW YORK

Sandy Creek
NEW YORK

An Imprint of Sterling Publishing
1166 Avenue of The Americas
New York, NY, 10036

ISBN 978-1-4351-5534-3

Manufactured in Guangdong, China
Lot #:
4 6 8 10 9 7 5 3
11/15

All images are courtesy of FLPA Images except for
page 48 (bottom) © Rolf Kopfle / ardea.com, page
102 © Jean Michel Labat / ardea.com and page 103
© David J. Green - animals / Alamy

Contents

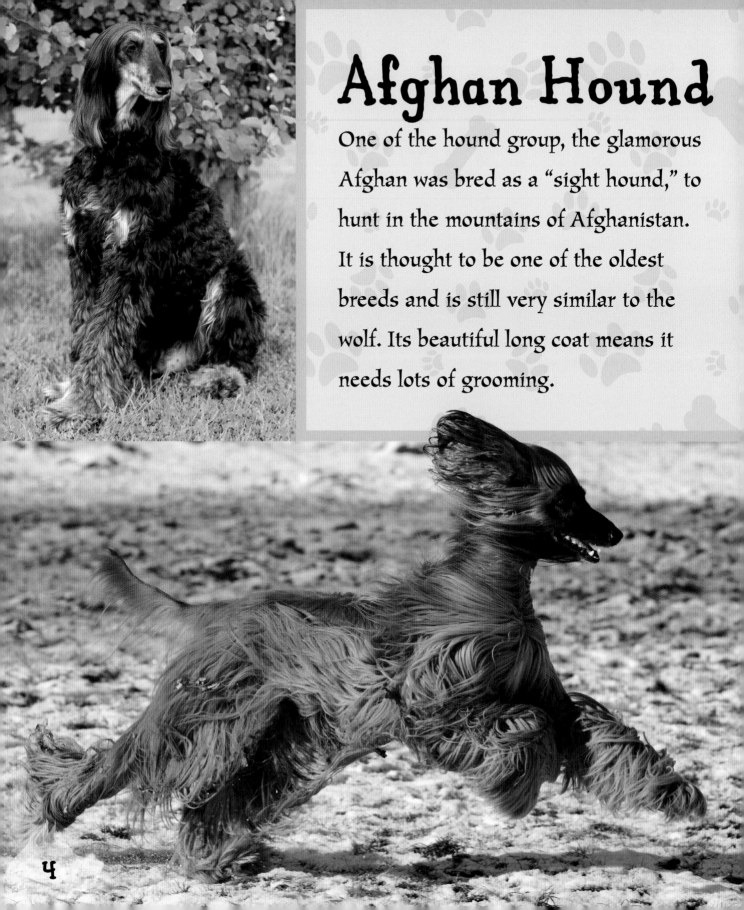

Afghan Hound

One of the hound group, the glamorous Afghan was bred as a "sight hound," to hunt in the mountains of Afghanistan. It is thought to be one of the oldest breeds and is still very similar to the wolf. Its beautiful long coat means it needs lots of grooming.

Airedale

This popular breed from the English county of Yorkshire is named after the River Aire. It's known as the "king of terriers," due to its size. In the First World War, it delivered messages behind enemy lines. It is sturdy and strong-minded, but very trainable.

7

Akita

In its native Japan, the Akita was used as a fighting dog and to hunt wild boar, deer, and black bears. The breed dates back around 300 years. There is now an American Akita, which is slightly bigger and heavier than the Japanese type.

American Cocker Spaniel

Although it is related to the English Cocker
Spaniel, the American version is a separate
breed. It has a luxurious long coat and
an enchanting face. Its delightful
and easy-going nature makes it
an ideal pet.

Basset Hound

In the Middle Ages monks bred this chunky little hound to hunt. Today, it makes an adorable pet. A Basset Hound has very long ears, called "leathers." It also has a very long body, which means several children can pet it at once!

Beagle

One of the most popular hound breeds, the Beagle was bred to hunt in a pack. They are intelligent dogs and make a wonderful family pet. It is lively and affectionate and always ready for action.

Bearded Collie

Dogs that were similar to today's Bearded Collie were found in Scotland 500 years ago. The modern "Beardie," as it is known today, has a lovely character and always looks like it wants to say, "What shall we do now?"

Bernese Mountain Dog

This breed dates back 2,000 years and was used in Switzerland for herding sheep and cattle, as well as pulling a small cart. It's had some rather unflattering names in the past, including "*Gelbbacken*" (Yellow Cheeks) and "*Vieraugen*" (Four Eyes).

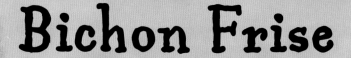

Bichon Frise

It is sometimes known as the "Tenerife dog" because sailors are thought to have found the breed on the island near Africa in the 14th century. It is a happy little character that loves attention, but needs lots of grooming.

Bloodhound

The Bloodhound was used to track criminals—it can follow a human scent for many hours and its deep, booming bark cannot be ignored. The breed is still used to find missing people and is often bred for that reason.

23

Border Collie

This breed is a herding "machine," used for gathering and moving sheep on hills and mountains. It works quickly and silently and responds instantly to every signal. Border Collies are also used as tracker and sniffer dogs.

25

Borzoi

The name of this breed means "swift" in its home country of Russia. It is also known as the Russian wolfhound. The beautiful Borzoi is built for speed and grace. It has a long, silky coat that easily gets tangled. Borzoi are quiet dogs and rarely bark.

27

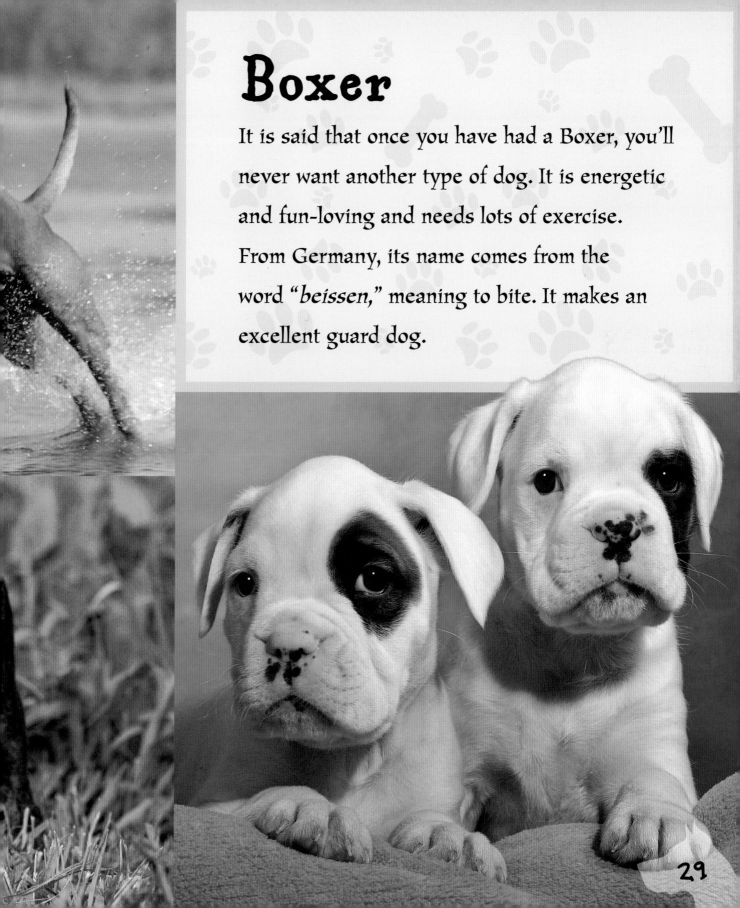

Boxer

It is said that once you have had a Boxer, you'll never want another type of dog. It is energetic and fun-loving and needs lots of exercise. From Germany, its name comes from the word "*beissen*," meaning to bite. It makes an excellent guard dog.

Briard

With its flowing coat made up of browns and black, the Briard is an extremely handsome dog. As well as its long fur, it has a beard, moustache, and eyebrows that all need regular grooming. It loves to play and is sweet-tempered and gentle.

31

Cavalier King Charles Spaniel

This spaniel is very similar to the King Charles Spaniel and the best way to describe both breeds is "happy." This compact little dog doesn't really mind what it does, as long as it is doing it with you! It makes a wonderful pet and a loyal friend.

Chihuahua

This charming breed takes its name from a state in Mexico, but has been made famous by pop stars and actresses as a "handbag dog." It is the smallest breed of dog in the world, but it doesn't know it—the cheeky Chihuahua has a big personality!

Chow Chow

The striking Chow Chow was originally only found in China so it was unknown to the rest of the world for a long time. It is strong and stocky and has an unusual blue/black tongue. It tends to prefer one person, rather than being a family pet.

37

Dachshund

The Dachshund was originally bred as a working dog in Germany. Despite its small size, it needs lots of exercise. There are three varieties: miniature long-haired, miniature short-haired, and wire-haired.

Dalmatian

The Dalmatian ran alongside horse-drawn carriages and ahead of fire engines in the past, earning the name "Firehouse dog." It is a friendly breed and loves human company. Puppies are born pure white and develop their spots later.

41

Doberman

A German tax collector named Karl Friedrich Louis Dobermann developed this breed because he needed a dog to protect him and persuade slow payers to hand over their money. The Doberman is an elegant, intelligent dog that is easy to train.

43

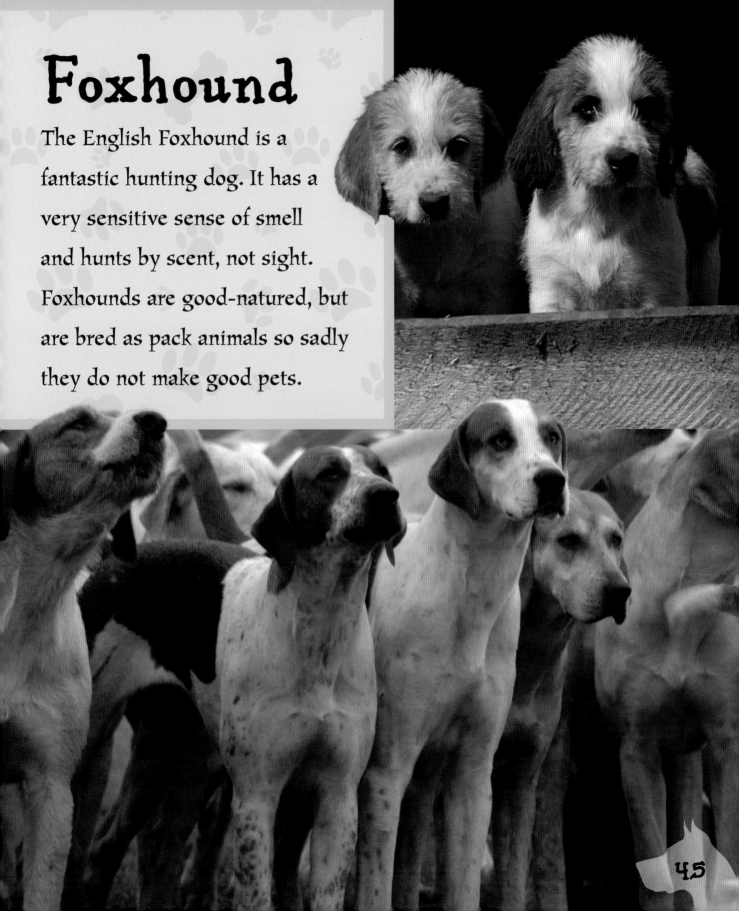

Foxhound

The English Foxhound is a fantastic hunting dog. It has a very sensitive sense of smell and hunts by scent, not sight. Foxhounds are good-natured, but are bred as pack animals so sadly they do not make good pets.

45

German Shepherd

The German Shepherd is very intelligent and was originally used for herding livestock. It is now used as a protection dog by the police, and as a seeing-eye dog. Its loyalty makes it a popular breed.

Golden Retriever

If ever one breed could sum up "man's best friend," it would be the Golden Retriever. This breed is always happy and good-humored. It is slow to mature, so it stays puppy-like and playful for many years.

Great Dane

Despite its huge size, the Great Dane is gentle and affectionate. It was once used to hunt wild boar, but makes an excellent guard dog as well as a loving family pet. Zeus is currently the tallest Great Dane, with a record-breaking height of 44 inches from paw to shoulder!

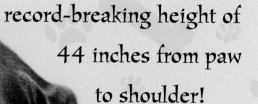

Greyhound

Drawings done thousands of years ago on the walls of tombs in Ancient Egypt look very much like the modern Greyhound. Today, it is used mostly as a racing dog. Only the speedy cheetah can match a Greyhound for speed.

Havanese

This lively little dog is the national dog of Cuba. It is also known as the Havana Silk Dog because of its gorgeous coat. Although it is small, the breed is not delicate and enjoys a bit of roughhousing.

55

56

Husky

Bred to pull sleds through the snow in Siberia and Alaska, the Husky is one of the most beautiful breeds. It has very unusual eyes—they can be brown or blue, or one of each. It also has a thick double coat. The Husky is friendly, but needs lots of exercise.

57

Irish Setter

If you want a glamorous pet, the Irish Setter is for you! It has a beautiful silky chestnut coat. It is good-tempered and will be loved by the whole family. This breed loves human company and will need regular long walks.

59

Irish Wolfhound

This mighty hound is the largest of all dog breeds. As its name suggests, it was originally bred to hunt wolves. When the last wolf in Ireland was killed around 1800, the breed almost died out. Today, however, the breed is thriving.

61

Jack Russell

This English breed was developed by the Reverend John Russell, a Victorian clergyman and a keen hunter. The Jack Russell is a very popular breed but there is also a shorter-legged variety: the Parson Russell Terrier.

Labrador

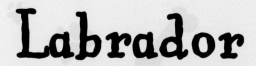

The Labrador was originally bred by fishermen, which means it is an excellent water dog. Its unusual tail is shaped like an otter's, and its smooth, flat coat is waterproof. It is now used to retrieve game rather than fish, but is also a very popular pet.

Lhasa Apso

The Lhaso Apso is from Tibet, a country with high mountains and harsh weather. Its long fur has a thick undercoat, which keeps it warm in freezing Tibetan winters. It also has hair over its eyes to protect them from wind, dust, and bright sunshine.

Malamute

This big dog was bred for strength—it was used to pull sleds in Alaska, pulling heavy loads over long distances. It is named after the Mahlemut tribe: hard-working people who were very proud of their handsome dogs.

Maltese

There is evidence that this dainty breed was found in Malta in Roman times. It was popular both as a lap dog and a "sleeve dog"—which means it was carried in the coat sleeve! Its dark eyes and nose stand out beautifully against its pure white coat.

Mastiff

When the Romans invaded Britain and discovered Mastiff-like dogs, they were so impressed they took them back to fight in the arenas of Rome. But the Mastiff is a gentle dog despite its size.

73

Newfoundland

A gentle giant, the huge Newfoundland is eager to please. As a puppy, it looks like a cuddly teddy bear, but grows quickly into a big, strong dog. It loves water and is a powerful swimmer, despite its long, thick coat.

75

76

Old English Sheepdog

With its long coat, the Old English Sheepdog takes a lot of grooming and it needs plenty of space to exercise. It makes a superb guard dog as it has a deep, booming bark to frighten off intruders, and is very protective.

Papillon

This tiny toy spaniel takes its name from the French word for "butterfly" because of the shape of its big, fringed ears. It is charming and intelligent and makes a delightful pet for the whole family. The Papillon loves to learn new tricks!

Pekingese

The Pekingese was so popular with the Imperial Court in ancient China that people were banned from owning one! Although it is small, it is said to have the heart of a lion and is also loving and playful.

Pinscher

Pinscher is the German word for "terrier," but this breed is much bigger than most terriers. It is a sturdy and elegant dog, and has a smooth, glossy coat. Obedient and responsive, the Pinscher makes an excellent guard dog.

Pomeranian

This dainty little dog has a fox-like face, a short body, and a thick, brush-like coat. It looks like a ball of fluff and has a sweet nature to match. The British monarch, Queen Victoria owned a Pomeranian, which increased the breed's popularity.

Pug

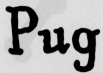

The Pug originally came from China where snub-nosed dogs have always been popular. Once just the pet of royalty, it is now popular all over the world. It is sociable and intelligent and lives to an old age.

Puli

It may sometimes be difficult to work out which direction the Puli is facing because of its wild and woolly coat! It was used as a herding dog in its original home of Hungary, so it needed all that fur to stay warm.

Pyrenees Mountain Dog

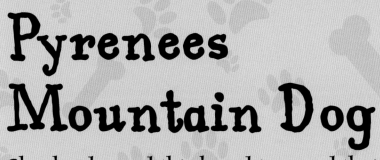

Shepherds used this breed to guard their sheep against wolves. However, it is a gentle and affectionate dog so it makes an excellent pet. It is not very active and doesn't need much exercise, but it does need a lot of grooming.

Rottweiler

Despite its fierce appearance, the Rottweiler is a trainable breed. It is not aggressive by nature but does have a rather "macho" image. It needs plenty of exercise and enjoys being a working dog. During both the World Wars, Rottweilers were used as messengers and as ambulance dogs collecting the wounded from the battlefields.

93

Saluki

The Saluki is one of the oldest domestic dog breeds. It was kept as a hunting dog in the Middle East and could move quickly over all types of ground. They can be difficult to train as they get bored easily.

95

Samoyed

Fur traders brought this enchanting breed to Great Britain from Siberia. Its thick coat gave it protection against the Siberian snow and ice. A charming dog, it always looks as if it is smiling. It is a lively breed and needs lots of exercise.

Schnauzer

In its native Germany, the Schnauzer was used to herd cattle and generally guard the house and stables. It could also pull a small cart, making it an all-round farm dog. A handsome animal, its wiry coat is often seen in "salt and pepper" shades. The Schnauzer makes a great pet.

Shar Pei

This unusual breed is originally from China. Western breeders tried to maximize the Shar Pei's wrinkled skin but this affected the dog's health. It is now generally less wrinkly and, despite its grumpy expression, is loving and loyal.

Shih Tzu

A gorgeous bundle of fluff, the Shih Tzu has a long, flowing coat, big dark eyes, and a curved tail. The name Shih Tzu comes from the Chinese word for lion. They are bouncy and friendly, and make loyal and loving pets.

Springer Spaniel

Springer Spaniels are gentle and loving and can be working dogs, show animals, or devoted pets. Originally hunting dogs, these spaniels were used to force game birds into the air by springing up and startling the birds. Springer Spaniels are friendly and easily excited.

St. Bernard

Its days as a rescue dog in the mountains of Switzerland may be over, but the massive and lovable St. Bernard makes a good pet. It takes a lot of grooming and, it has to be said, produces a fair amount of slobber!

107

Staffordshire Bull Terrier

A very popular breed, the Staffy is a cross between a Bulldog and a terrier. Although the Staffordshire Bull can have a bad reputation, it is affectionate and good with children. It doesn't need lots of exercise or grooming.

109

Standard Poodle

There are three sizes of poodle—standard, toy, and miniature. It is a born entertainer and used to perform in circuses in France. The breed is thought to have come from Germany, where it was used to retrieve game.

Vizsla

In its home country of Hungary, the Vizsla was used as a gundog. It was happy working in all weathers. It is good-looking and intelligent, which makes it an easy breed to train. The Vizsla makes a lively and loving pet.

Weimaraner

With its pinkish-grey coloring and light amber or blue-grey eyes, the striking Weimaraner has become a popular pet. As one of the larger breeds, it does need lots of exercise and space. Weimaraners enjoy being part of a family and especially love children.

Welsh Corgi

There are two types of Welsh Corgi—the Cardigan and the Pembroke. The breed was once known as the Yard Dog, because the length from the tip of the dog's nose to the end of its tail is the same as the measurement for a Welsh yard.

West Highland White Terrier

Full of fun and almost tireless, the West Highland Terrier makes a wonderful pet. It's always ready for a walk, but its small size means it can be picked up and carried anywhere. It is a friendly and happy little dog.

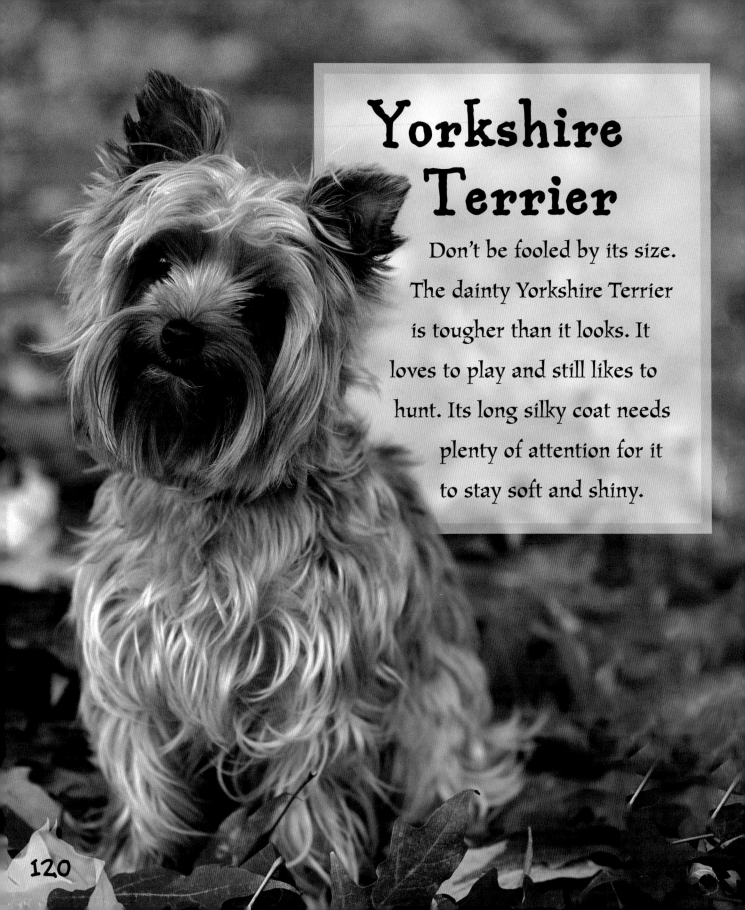

Yorkshire Terrier

Don't be fooled by its size. The dainty Yorkshire Terrier is tougher than it looks. It loves to play and still likes to hunt. Its long silky coat needs plenty of attention for it to stay soft and shiny.